Scott Foresman

Classroom Management Handbook for Differentiated Instruction Practice Stations

Glenview, Illinois • Boston, Massachusetts • Chandler, Arizona • Upper Saddle River, New Jersey

ISBN-13: 978-0-328-47771-5
ISBN-10: 0-328-47771-0

6 7 8 9 10 V063 14 13 12

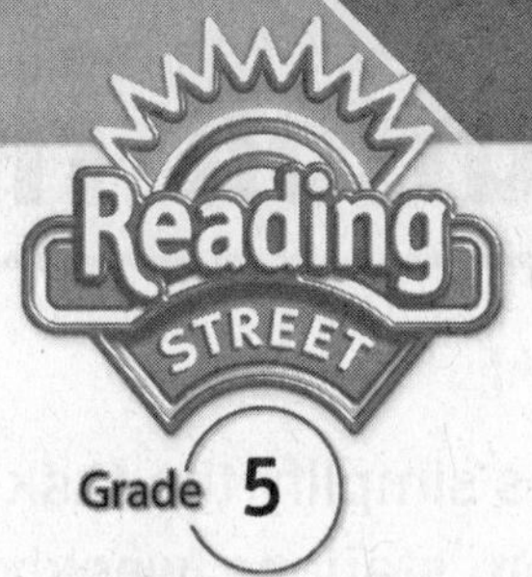

Table of Contents

Welcome to Station Time!

Practice Stations Kit

The Leveled Practice Stations Kit helps simplify the task of managing stations by providing ideas for setting up classroom stations, weekly activities for each station, and suggested materials for each station.

Classroom Management Handbook for Differentiated Instruction Practice Stations

The Management Handbook provides valuable resources to help you set up practice stations and to provide differentiated practice that enables you to address students at their instructional levels while they are working independently. The Scott Foresman Differentiated Instruction Practice Stations help students develop as independent thinkers who take responsibility for their own learning. The Handbook provides a suggested classroom floor plan that can be adjusted to fit the particular needs of your classroom. An overview for each station provides suggestions for setting up the stations and essential materials to include. The reproducible Student Work Plans list tasks that students will complete at each station and help students plan and track their assignments at each station.

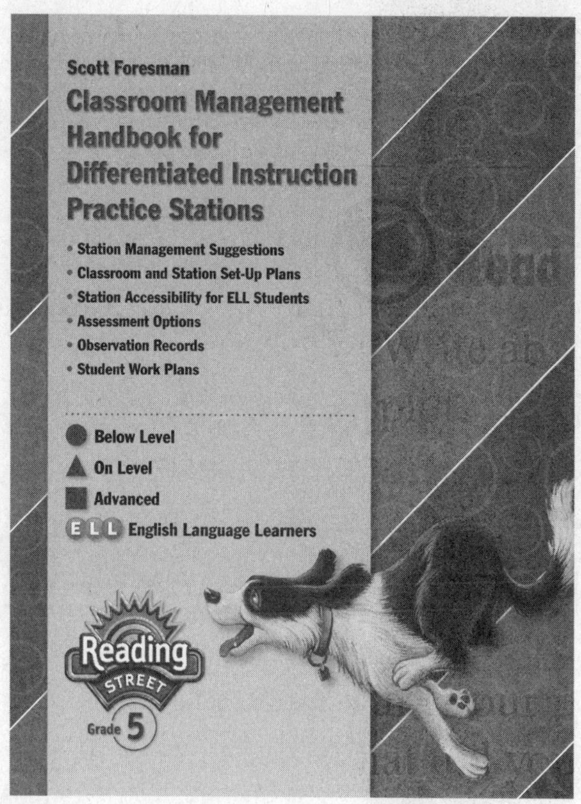

Practice Station Flip Charts

The Practice Stations Flip Charts are tabletop-sized flip charts with the Practice Stations activities from the Teacher's Edition. Each flip-chart page provides the weekly differentiated activities for that station. The activities provide opportunities for students to practice skills and to expand knowledge of the weekly concept. There are six flip charts, one for each station.

- Word Wise (spelling station)
- Word Work (phonics station)
- Works to Know (vocabulary station)

- Let's Write! (writing station)
- Read for Meaning (comprehension station)
- Get Fluent (fluency station)

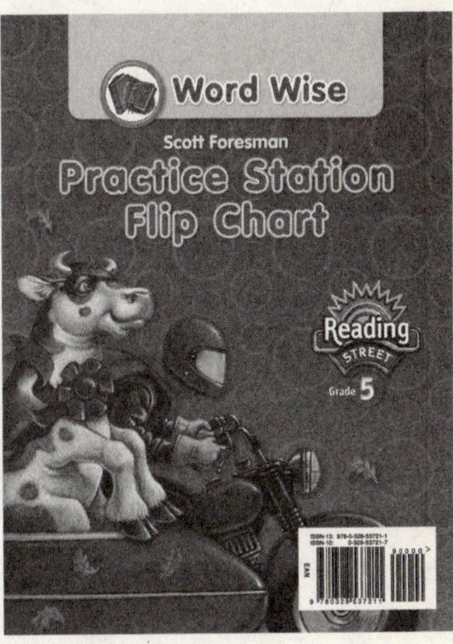

Setting Up the Stations

The classroom environment is an important factor in students' learning. To help create a comfortable environment that is conducive to learning, create separate spaces for the different types of instruction and activities that take place each day.

A Station-Friendly Classroom

As much as possible, a classroom environment should be warm, inviting, and conducive to effective learning for you and your students. As an integral part of that environment, cross-curricular stations should be comfortable areas in which students can work independently, in pairs, or in small groups. To that end, consider some or all of the following suggestions when developing your stations.

- Set aside an area for whole-class instruction and a space for you to work with small groups.
- Think about the function of each station and where it is most appropriately located in the room.
- Provide as much space as possible between noisy and quiet areas.
- Develop traffic patterns that allow for easy movement through and around stations.

One possible classroom setup is shown to the right.

Establish Stations Routines

Station time will be most effective if you develop routines and set clear expectations for students working in the stations. The goal is to enable students to work independently. Following are suggestions to help students reach independence.

- At the beginning of the year, model how to use the stations and coach students on how to be responsible when working in the stations.
- Establish rules for each station, discuss these with students, and post them in the stations.
- Make sure that students understand what is expected of them for each station activity. Post suggestions for early finishers in each station.
- Support students in making their own decisions about what to do at a station and how to solve problems.
- Use a management chart so that students will know where they should be on a daily basis.
- Appoint a "stations monitor" each week whose job it is to update the management chart and make sure that students know where they should be working.
- Distribute copies of "My Work Plan" each week to help students plan their time and tasks.
- Stock each station with appropriate supplies.

Once students are using the stations, you can rotate among them, answering questions, providing direction, guiding research, and assessing performance.

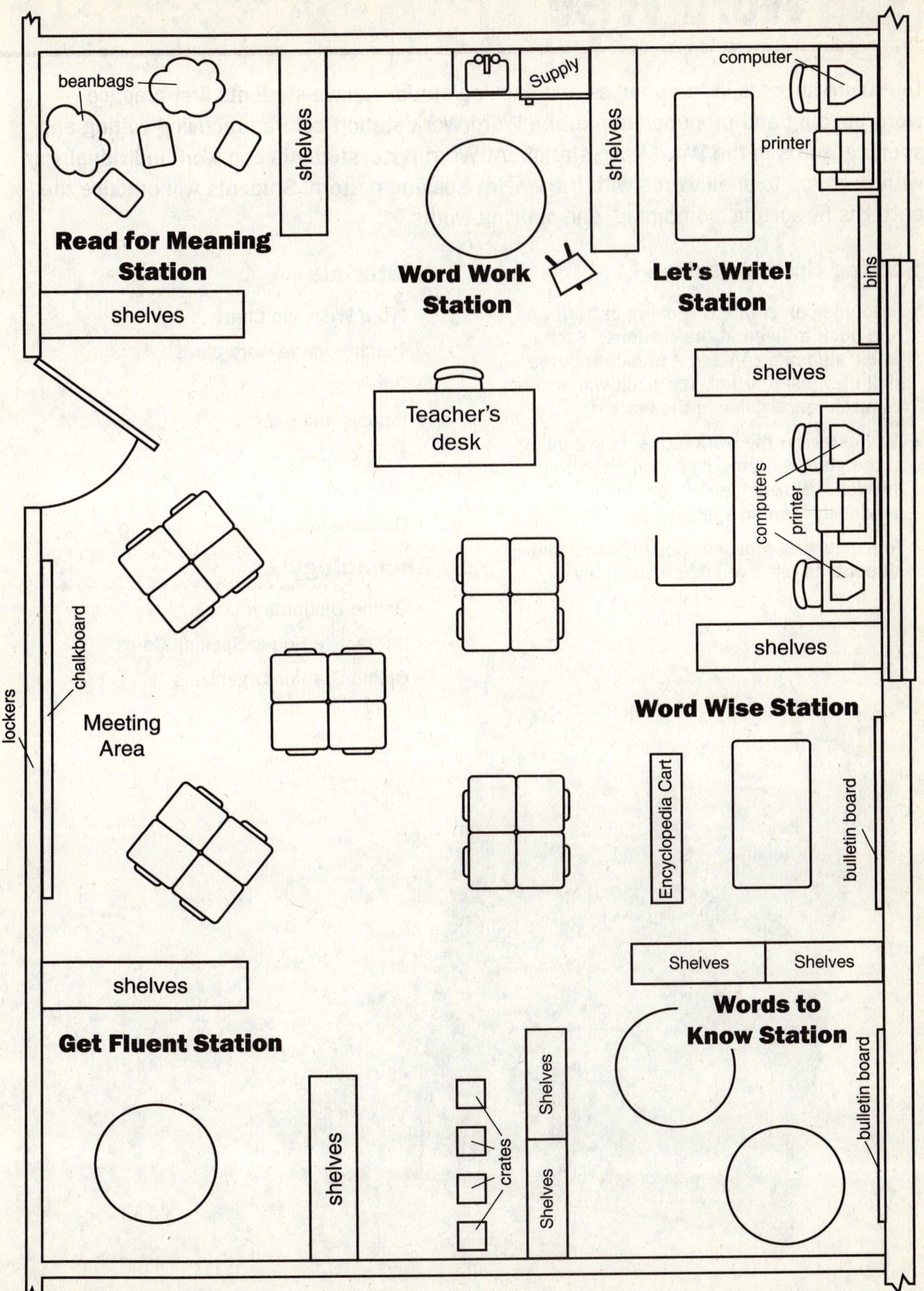

beanbags
Read for Meaning Station
shelves
shelves
Supply
Word Work Station
computer
printer
Let's Write! Station
bins
shelves
Teacher's desk
computers
printer
chalkboard
lockers
Meeting Area
Word Wise Station
Encyclopedia Cart
bulletin board
shelves
Shelves
Shelves
shelves
Get Fluent Station
shelves
crates
Shelves
Shelves
Words to Know Station
bulletin board

Word Wise

To ensure success in the phonics and spelling stations, have students first practice word building and pronunciation in the Word Work station before practicing writing and spelling words in the Word Wise station. At Word Wise, students can work individually or with partners to spell words with the weekly spelling pattern. Students will practice the patterns by sorting, combining, and spelling words.

Setting Up the Station

- Students can create a spelling pattern and rule book to keep at the stations. Each week, students can add a page about the skill they just learned. The book will also act as a reference guide in the station.

- As you review the work students are doing in the stations, look to see whether they are demonstrating an understanding of previously learned spelling skills.

- To review and practice spelling skills, allow students to use available technology.

Materials

- *Word Wise* Flip Chart
- Teacher-made word cards
- Paper
- Pencils and pens
- Note cards
- Graphic organizers
- Dictionaries

Technology

- Online Dictionary
- Interactive Sound-Spelling Cards
- Online Graphic Organizers

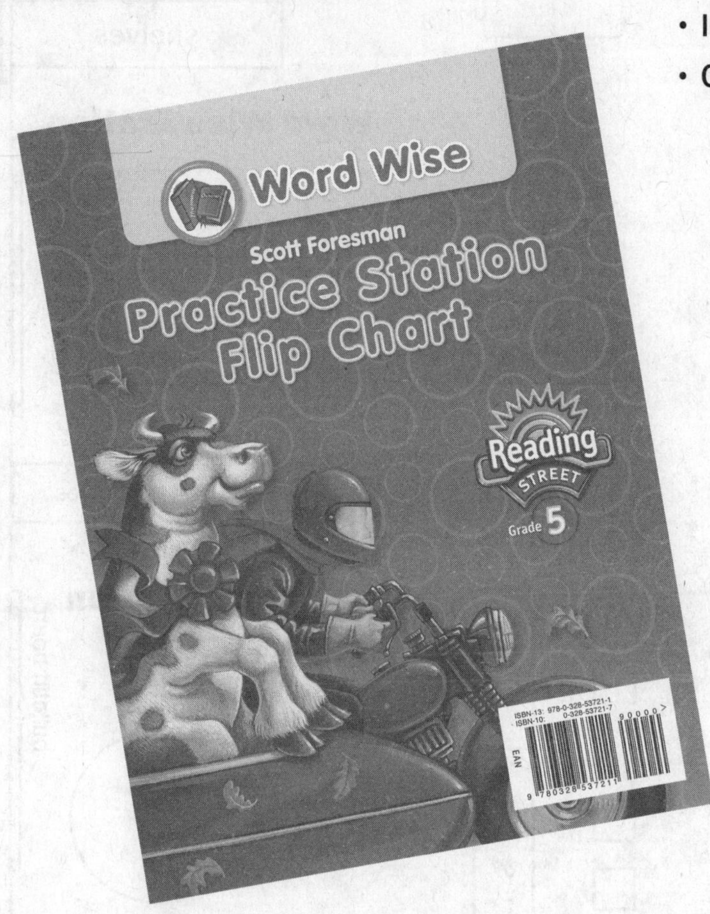

Word Work

At Word Work students can work individually or with partners to identify, build, and pronounce words to practice the phonics and spelling skill. Once students demonstrate an understanding of the skill, they are ready to move to Word Wise to practice spelling and writing words with the same spelling skill.

Setting Up the Station

Provide a table or group of desks where students can work individually and in pairs.

- Students can create a pronunciation chart or book to keep at the station. Each week, students can add a page about the skill they just learned. The book will also act as a reference guide in the station.

- As time allows, listen to see that students are building and pronouncing new and learned words correctly. Model correct pronunciation as needed.

- To review and practice spelling skills, allow students to use available technology.

- Allow students to listen to the Modeled Pronunciation Audio CD for additional practice with letter-sound relationships.

Materials

- *Word Work* Flip Chart
- Teacher-made word cards
- Paper
- Pencils and pens
- Note cards

Technology

- Modeled Pronunciation Audio CD
- Online Graphic Organizers

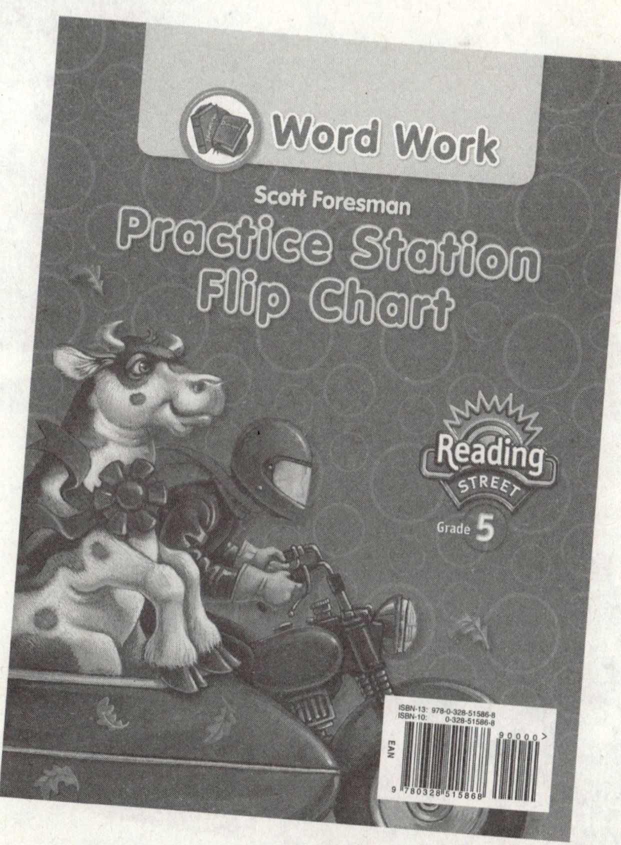

Words to Know

At Words to Know, the vocabulary station, students will use the lesson vocabulary strategies and word analysis skills to extend and enrich their understanding of key concepts and themes. Students will also build their speaking and reading vocabularies.

Setting Up the Station

Provide a table or group of desks where students can work individually or in pairs.

- Supplement the station with additional vocabulary-building activities that are language-rich.
- Use lesson vocabulary and weekly spelling words with these activities to practice strategies and reinforce understanding of word meanings.

Materials

- *Words to Know* Flip Chart
- Teacher-made word cards
- Paper
- Pencils, pens
- Dictionaries, thesauruses

Technology

- Envision It! Pictured Vocabulary Cards
- Online Dictionary
- Vocabulary Activities

Let's Write!

Let's Write!, the writing station, allows students to work on a variety of writing activities. These activities provide opportunities for students to extend concepts learned while writing in multiple genres.

Setting Up the Station

The writing station may need more space than other stations.

- Designate a table for students who are working on prewriting and drafting activities, and another for revising, editing, and publishing.
- Set up computers for word processing on another table or on a group of desks.
- Stock the station with any necessary writing materials. Include the weekly list of spelling words, vocabulary words, and the Amazing Words to provide practice.

Materials

- *Let's Write!* Flip Chart
- Paper
- Pencils, pens
- Dictionaries, thesauruses
- Graphic organizers
- Revising and editing checklists

Technology

- Online Graphic Organizers
- Online Journal
- Grammar Jammer
- Online Dictionary

Read for Meaning

At Read for Meaning, the reading comprehension station, students can read additional materials to practice target comprehension skills and strategies. They can also make connections across texts, explore personal interests, or find out more about topics, authors, and genres that are related to the week's concept.

Setting Up the Station

Find a comfortable space for this station away from the main activity of the classroom.

- Include a table and chairs as well as rocking chairs, carpet squares, or beanbags.
- Use shelves, wire rack bins, or plastic tote trays to create an organized classroom library.
- Group books by theme, topic, genre, reading level, or author.

Materials

- *Read for Meaning* Flip Chart
- Leveled Readers
- Paper
- Pencils, pens
- Graphic organizers

Technology

- Leveled Reader Database
- Reading Street Leveled Readers CD-ROM
- Envision It! Animations
- Main and Paired eSelections
- Online Graphic Organizers

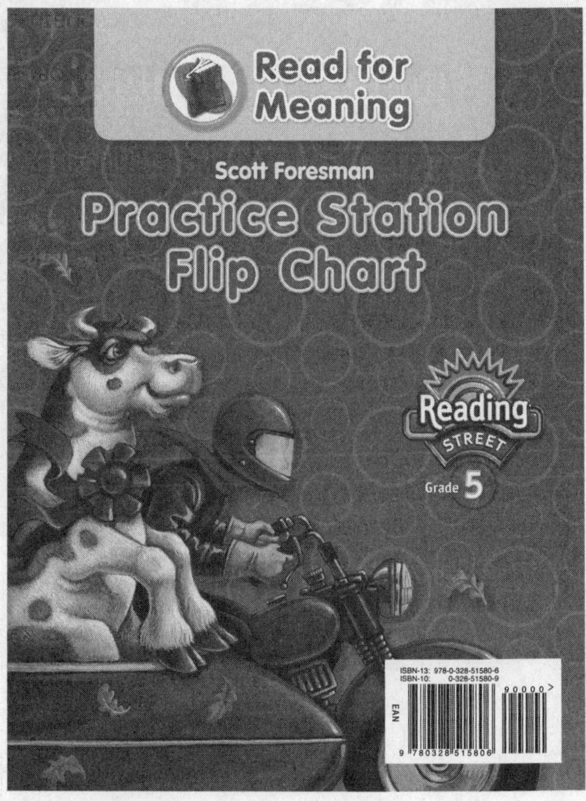

Get Fluent

Get Fluent, the fluency station, is the place where students practice fluent reading. Students will listen to and read aloud various texts while focusing on reading with accuracy, at an appropriate rate, with appropriate phrasing, and with expression and intonation.

Setting Up the Station

Students will often read with a partner. Set up this station where the students' work will be the least disruptive to other classmates.

- Locate the station near a computer so students can utilize available technology.

- Provide headsets so that students listening to audio will not be distracted by other noises.

- Arrange the table and chairs to allow partners to work together easily.

- Occasionally reassign partners in order to provide students with a variety of fluency models and partner feedback.

Materials

- *Get Fluent* Flip Chart
- Leveled Readers
- CD player

Technology

- Leveled Reader Database

- Reading Street Leveled Readers CD-ROM

- AudioText CD

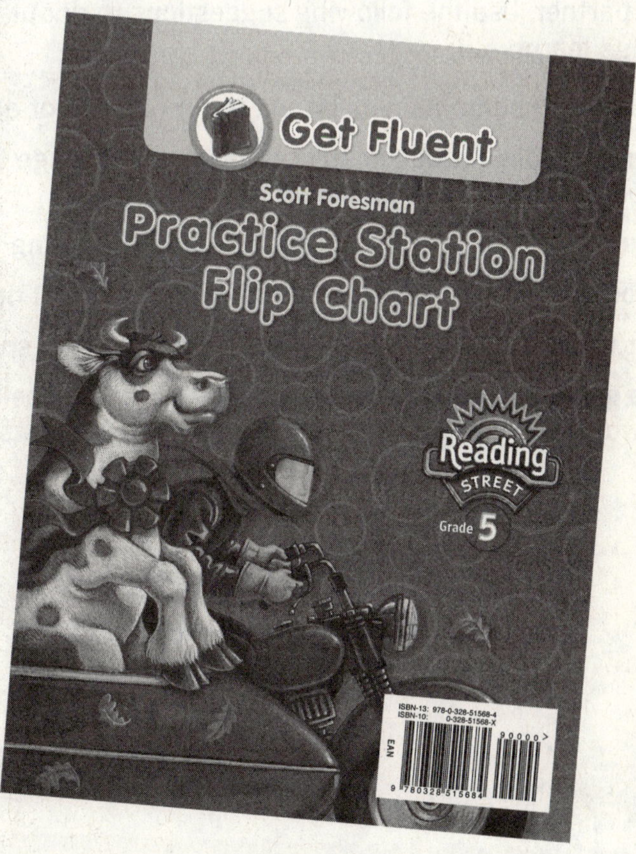

ELL-Accessible Stations

The *Scott Foresman Practice Stations* can be adapted to be more accessible to English language learners. Frontloading suggestions and background building information found in the core lesson help support all of the independent activities in the stations. Modeling with picture cues, real objects, and role-playing can help English language learners understand what they need to do without solely depending on language. Students should be encouraged to listen, speak, read, and write during their time in each station. Enhance language production by structuring cooperative learning opportunities at the Practice Stations. Pair students who share the same home language, or have more proficient students work with newcomers. This extra support provides a positive example and support for completing activities in the stations. The stations provide an environment where students can feel comfortable practicing English without worrying about errors they may make.

Word Wise and Word Work

Word Wise and Word Work, the spelling and phonics stations, practice the same set of skills each week, so the stations can be adapted in similar ways. Encourage students to decode the words aloud with a partner. Use the following suggestions to adapt the spelling and phonics stations for English language learners.

- Be sure that students understand the meanings of all of the words before they use the station.
- When possible, introduce any cognates or language transfer skills that will help students better understand the words practiced.
- Review the spelling words or spelling patterns using the Sound-Spelling Charts.
- Use one of the teacher-made word cards to model decoding the spelling pattern.
- Point to the spellings of the word as you say each sound. Model blending each word.
- Have groups of mixed abilities use letter tiles to spell out the spelling words. Students should read the words they made to the other groups of students. Offer guidance as necessary.

Words to Know

English language learners can benefit in Words to Know by using visuals and real objects to scaffold meaning. Encourage students to use their home languages to transfer any knowledge or strategies to what they are practicing. The following suggestions can be used to adapt the vocabulary station.

- Introduce any cognates or language transfer skills that will help students better understand the lesson vocabulary.
- Revisit the lesson vocabulary words with students daily. Help students say each word and encourage oral production.
- Review any suffixes, prefixes, word endings, or word origins students may encounter in the weekly lesson vocabulary.
- Have groups of mixed abilities work together using letter tiles to spell their lesson vocabulary words. Have more advanced students model and define the words.

Let's Write!

Students at all proficiency levels should be given a variety of materials they need to be able to write successfully. Some students may benefit from brainstorming and using graphic organizers while some may benefit by working independently with a writing prompt. The adaptations below may help your English language learners succeed in the writing station.

- Provide sentence frames, writing prompts, or writing models to assist students' writing.
- For beginning and intermediate students, write out sentences they dictate. Allow them to copy the sentences and then read them aloud to you.
- More advanced students can write sentences and share with a partner.

Read for Meaning

Have a variety of ELL and ELD Readers available at Read for Meaning. Students may benefit from reviewing the comprehension skill with the Envision It! illustrations in the Student Edition or the Picture It! blackline masters found in the *English Language Learner's Handbook*. The station may be adapted using the following suggestions.

- When possible, use picture cues to review the comprehension skill.
- Choose a selection that is appropriate to students' reading level. Read aloud the selection with the students.
- During reading, ask questions or fill out a graphic organizer with students to monitor their comprehension.
- Allow beginning and intermediate students to orally explain the relationships between the comprehension skill and the selection read. More advanced students can complete this activity by writing sentences.

Get Fluent

Guide students to determine the best fluency routine for them to use at this station. Be sure all students are practicing the different fluency traits with texts at their level and that they understand what they are reading. Adapt the fluency station using the following suggestions.

- Have pairs of mixed-ability students reread the ELL or ELD Reader to each other.
- Circulate and evaluate intermediate to advanced students for word recognition, accuracy, and prosody.
- Work individually with beginning and intermediate students, focusing on decoding for meaning. Provide support as needed.

The Practice Stations provide valuable opportunities for students to gain knowledge and increase their confidence, thereby making their social and academic classroom experiences more meaningful. In addition, students' involvement in the stations will strengthen their performance in all areas of instruction, and their work in the stations will positively affect their ability to function as active and independent learners.

Assessment

Station activities provide excellent opportunities for informal, ongoing assessments that are useful in guiding instruction. Effective station activities provide opportunities for students to engage in meaningful tasks that advance learning in all areas, especially reading and writing. Emphasize to students that activities completed in the stations are important and will be assessed. Use information gathered from these assessments to guide instruction for individuals, groups, or the entire class.

Assessment Suggestions

Observe Student Work

- Determine what you expect in terms of student behaviors and attitudes and develop checklists based on those expectations.

- Focus on one or more students each day and keep informal notes about behavior, motivation, performance, or any other information you think is significant.

- Document students' learning and work habits and record social interactions.

- Hold periodic, structured conferences with students about their work.

- Plan support that addresses a student's particular strength or need.

- Record any information that will help make instructional decisions. You may want to use the Observation Record on page 17.

Create and Post Rubrics

- Create a rubric to assess how well students follow station directions.

- Use a rubric to assess student creativity and motivation.

- Post a rubric in Let's Write!, the writing station, so that students are aware of assessment criteria for writing projects.

Establish Portfolios

- Help students establish portfolios for station activities in progress.

- Use portfolio contents as a measure of progress and growth over time.

Involve Students in Self-Assessments

- Have students evaluate their own work and set goals for improvement.

- Have students evaluate each other's work in pairs and groups.

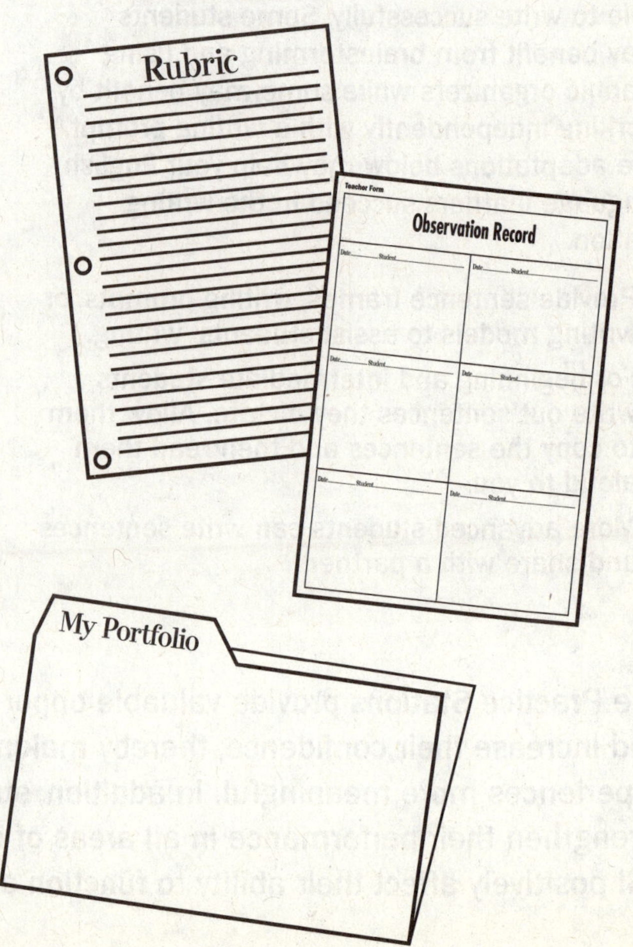

Observation Record

Date.................. Student..

Date.................. Student..

Date.................. Student..

Date.................. Student..

Date.................. Student..

Date.................. Student..

Student Work Plans

What Are Student Work Plans?

Pages 19–48 contain lesson-specific reproducible work plans for students to use during their independent activity time. Each work plan lists the tasks that students will complete, in stations or independently, while you meet with small groups. The work plans help students remember their assignments, plan their time, and keep track of what they've done. Work plans allow students to take responsibility and will aid them in becoming successful independent learners.

How Do I Use the Student Work Plans?

Begin by explaining the activities in the Practice Stations to students. Then distribute copies of *My Work Plan* and review the tasks. Be sure students understand that they will check the box next to each task as they complete it. Remind students that if they finish an activity before time is up, they should answer the Wrap Up Your Week questions or read silently. At the end of the week, you can collect students' work plans, or you can send them home.

If you prefer, you can customize a work plan for one or more students or for use during a particular lesson. For this purpose, a generic work plan can be found on p. 49.

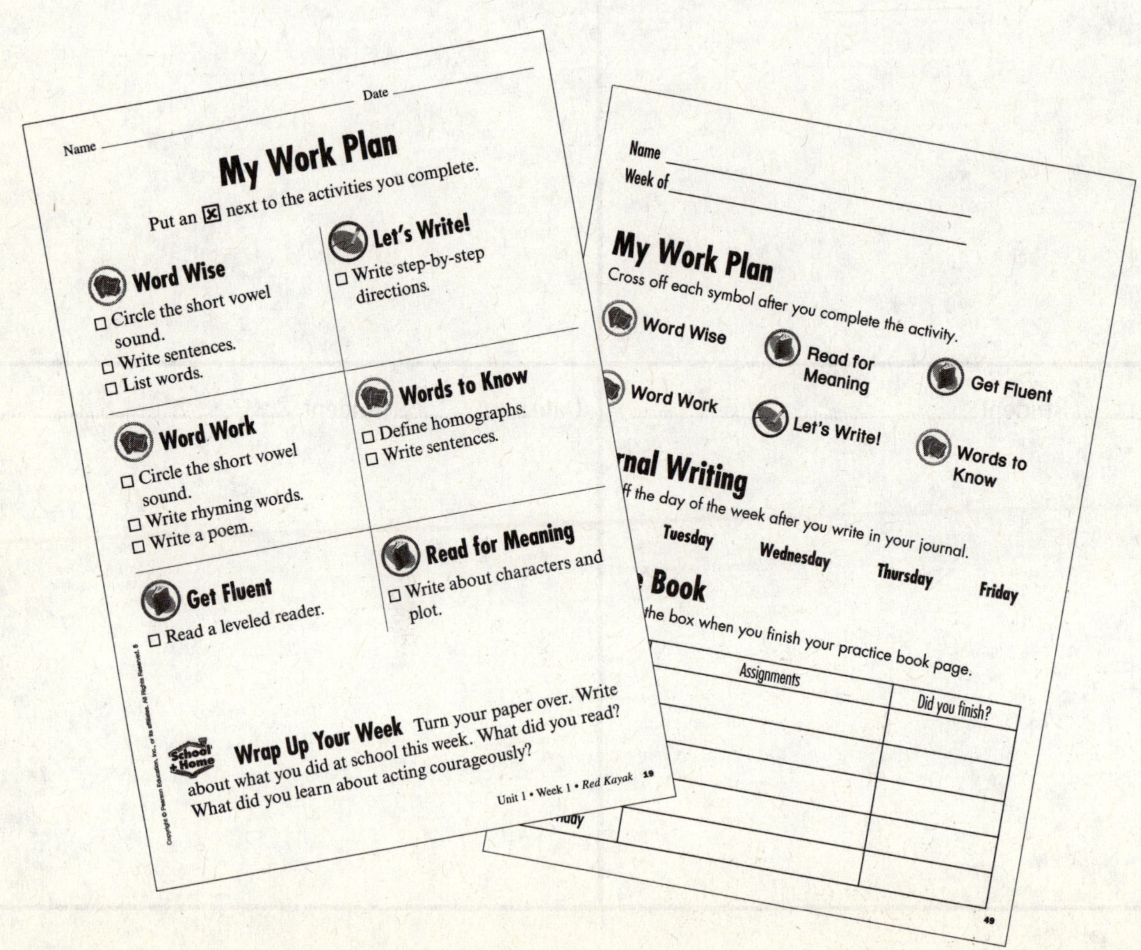

My Work Plan

Put an ☒ next to the activities you complete.

Word Wise

- ☐ Circle the short vowel sound.
- ☐ Write sentences.
- ☐ List words.

Let's Write!

- ☐ Write step-by-step directions.

Word Work

- ☐ Circle the short vowel sound.
- ☐ Write rhyming words.
- ☐ Write a poem.

Words to Know

- ☐ Define homographs.
- ☐ Write sentences.

Get Fluent

- ☐ Read a leveled reader.

Read for Meaning

- ☐ Write about characters and plot.

School + Home

Wrap Up Your Week Turn your paper over. Write about what you did at school this week. What did you read? What did you learn about acting courageously?

My Work Plan

Put an ☒ next to the activities you complete.

Word Wise

- ☐ Circle the short vowel sound.
- ☐ Write sentences.
- ☐ List words.

Let's Write!

- ☐ Write step-by-step instructions.

Word Work

- ☐ Circle the short vowel sound.
- ☐ Write rhyming words.
- ☐ Write a poem.

Words to Know

- ☐ Define homographs.
- ☐ Write sentences.

Get Fluent

- ☐ Read a leveled reader.

Read for Meaning

- ☐ Write about characters and plot.

School + Home **Wrap Up Your Week** Turn your paper over. Write about what you did at school. What did you read? What did you learn about challenges in nature?

My Work Plan

Put an ☒ next to the activities you complete.

Word Wise

☐ Circle the long vowel sound.
☐ Write sentences.
☐ List words.

Let's Write!

☐ Write a tall tale.
☐ Include exaggeration.

Word Work

☐ List words with long vowel sounds.
☐ Write sentences.

Words to Know

☐ Define homonyms.
☐ Write sentences.

Get Fluent

☐ Read a leveled reader.

Read for Meaning

☐ Use a graphic organizer.
☐ List causes and effects.

Wrap Up Your Week Turn your paper over. Write about what you did at school. What did you read? What did you learn about survival?

My Work Plan

Put an ☒ next to the activities you complete.

 ## Word Wise

- ☐ Circle the long vowel sound.
- ☐ Write sentences.
- ☐ List words.

 ## Let's Write!

- ☐ Write a letter or an invitation.

 ## Word Work

- ☐ Circle the long vowel sound.
- ☐ List words.

 ## Words to Know

- ☐ Define unknown words.
- ☐ Write sentences.

 ## Get Fluent

- ☐ Read a leveled reader.

 ## Read for Meaning

- ☐ Write about the theme and setting.

Wrap Up Your Week Turn your paper over. Write about what you did at school. What did you read? What did you learn about personal challenges?

My Work Plan

Put an ☒ next to the activities you complete.

 ## Word Wise

- ☐ Circle base words.
- ☐ Write sentences.
- ☐ Write other forms of words.

 ## Let's Write!

- ☐ Write a newsletter article.

 ## Word Work

- ☐ Sort words in a chart.

 ## Words to Know

- ☐ List antonyms.
- ☐ Write sentences.

 ## Get Fluent

- ☐ Read a leveled reader.

 ## Read for Meaning

- ☐ Write facts and opinions.

Wrap Up Your Week Turn your paper over. Write about what you did at school. What did you read? What did you learn about life in a new country?

My Work Plan

Put an ☒ next to the activities you complete.

 ## Word Wise

☐ Write words that form contractions.
☐ Write sentences.

 ## Let's Write!

☐ Write a problem-solution composition.

 ## Word Work

☐ List contractions.
☐ Write sentences.

 ## Words to Know

☐ Define multiple-meaning words.
☐ Write sentences.

 ## Get Fluent

☐ Read a leveled reader.

 ## Read for Meaning

☐ Write causes and effects.

Wrap Up Your Week Turn your paper over. Write about what you did at school. What did you read? What did you learn about honesty?

My Work Plan

Put an ⊠ next to the activities you complete.

Word Wise

- ☐ Circle the digraphs.
- ☐ Write sentences.
- ☐ List words.

Let's Write!

- ☐ Write a description.

Word Work

- ☐ List words.
- ☐ Circle the digraphs.
- ☐ Sort words into a chart.

Words to Know

- ☐ Define unfamiliar words.
- ☐ Write sentences or a paragraph.

Get Fluent

- ☐ Read a leveled reader.

Read for Meaning

- ☐ Compare and contrast characters.

Wrap Up Your Week Turn your paper over. Write about what you did at school. What did you read? What did you learn about taking risks?

My Work Plan

Put an ⊠ next to the activities you complete.

 ## Word Wise

☐ Write sentences.
☐ Write the singular form of words.

 ## Let's Write!

☐ Write a friendly letter.

 ## Word Work

☐ List irregular plurals.
☐ Write a poem.

 ## Words to Know

☐ Define unknown words.
☐ List parts of speech.
☐ Write sentences.

 ## Get Fluent

☐ Read a leveled reader.

 ## Read for Meaning

☐ Write the sequence of events.

Wrap Up Your Week Turn your paper over. Write about what you did at school. What did you read? What did you learn about helping others?

My Work Plan

Put an ☒ next to the activities you complete.

 ## Word Wise

- ☐ Circle *r*-controlled vowels.
- ☐ Write sentences.
- ☐ List words.

 ## Let's Write!

- ☐ Write a poem.

 ## Word Work

- ☐ List words.
- ☐ Group words in a chart by sound.

 ## Words to Know

- ☐ Circle Greek or Latin roots.
- ☐ Write sentences.
- ☐ List words.

 ## Get Fluent

- ☐ Read a leveled reader.

 ## Read for Meaning

- ☐ Compare and contrast characters.

Wrap Up Your Week Turn your paper over. Write about what you did at school. What did you read? What did you learn about making sacrifices?

My Work Plan

Put an ☒ next to the activities you complete.

 ## Word Wise

- ☐ Underline the final syllable.
- ☐ Write sentences.
- ☐ List words.

 ## Let's Write!

- ☐ Write a personal narrative.

 ## Word Work

- ☐ Group words by final syllables.
- ☐ Write sentences.

 ## Words to Know

- ☐ Use context clues to define unfamiliar words.
- ☐ List parts of speech.
- ☐ Write sentences.

 ## Get Fluent

- ☐ Read a leveled reader.

 ## Read for Meaning

- ☐ Write the author's purpose.
- ☐ Use supporting details.

Wrap Up Your Week Turn your paper over. Write about what you did at school. What did you read? What did you learn about promoting freedom?

My Work Plan

Put an ☒ next to the activities you complete.

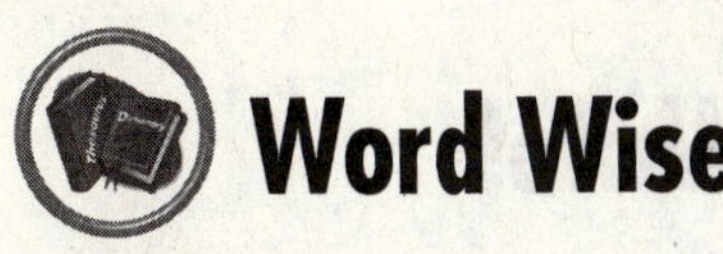 ## Word Wise

☐ Spell words.
☐ Underline the final syllable.
☐ Write sentences.

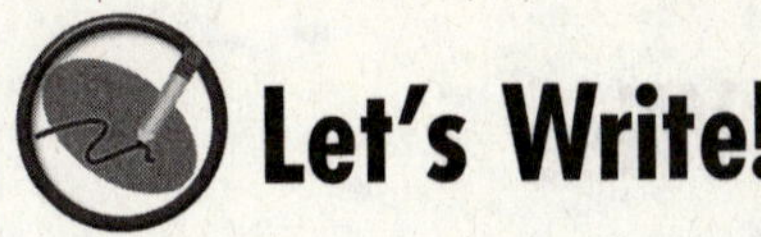 ## Let's Write!

☐ Write historical fiction.

 ## Word Work

☐ List words with final syllables.

 ## Words to Know

☐ Add endings to base words.
☐ Write sentences.

 ## Get Fluent

☐ Read a leveled reader.

 ## Read for Meaning

☐ Write the author's purpose.
☐ Use supporting details.

Wrap Up Your Week Turn your paper over. Write about what you did at school. What did you read? What did you learn about inventors and imaginations?

My Work Plan

Put an ☒ next to the activities you complete.

 ## Word Wise

☐ Underline the schwa sound.
☐ Write sentences or a paragraph.

 ## Let's Write!

☐ Write a play.
☐ Include dialogue.

 ## Word Work

☐ Circle the schwa sound.
☐ List words.

 ## Words to Know

☐ Define multiple-meaning words.
☐ Write sentences.

 ## Get Fluent

☐ Read a leveled reader.

 ## Read for Meaning

☐ Write the sequence of events.

School + Home **Wrap Up Your Week** Turn your paper over. Write about what you did at school. What did you read? What did you learn about art and artists?

My Work Plan

Put an ☒ next to the activities you complete.

 ## Word Wise

☐ Write words that form compound words.
☐ Write sentences.

 ## Let's Write!

☐ Write a persuasive speech.

 ## Word Work

☐ Circle words that form compound words.
☐ List compound words.

 ## Words to Know

☐ Identify the Greek or Latin root.
☐ Write sentences.
☐ List words.

 ## Get Fluent

☐ Read a leveled reader.

 ## Read for Meaning

☐ Write the main idea.
☐ Use supporting details.

Wrap Up Your Week Turn your paper over. Write about what you did at school. What did you read? What did you learn about dinosaurs and paleontology?

My Work Plan

Put an ☒ next to the activities you complete.

Word Wise

- ☐ List words.
- ☐ Write sentences.

Let's Write!

- ☐ Write and illustrate an advertisement.

Word Work

- ☐ Circle the consonant sounds.
- ☐ Sort words in a chart.

Words to Know

- ☐ Define homonyms.
- ☐ Write sentences.

Get Fluent

- ☐ Read a leveled reader.

Read for Meaning

- ☐ Write facts and opinions.

Wrap Up Your Week Turn your paper over. Write about what you did at school. What did you read? What did you learn about music and musicians?

My Work Plan

Put an ☒ next to the activities you complete.

 ## Word Wise

☐ Write sentences.
☐ List words.

 ## Let's Write!

☐ Write a description of your favorite meal.

 ## Word Work

☐ Circle double consonants.
☐ Write rhyming words.
☐ Write a poem.

 ## Words to Know

☐ Identify an antonym.
☐ Write sentences.

 ## Get Fluent

☐ Read a leveled reader.

 ## Read for Meaning

☐ Write the main idea.
☐ Use supporting details.

Wrap Up Your Week Turn your paper over. Write about what you did at school. What did you read? What did you learn about special effects?

My Work Plan

Put an ☒ next to the activities you complete.

Word Wise

☐ Circle prefixes.
☐ Write sentences.

Let's Write!

☐ Write a composition comparing two things.

Word Work

☐ Sort words in a chart.

Words to Know

☐ Define words with prefixes.
☐ Write sentences.

Get Fluent

☐ Read a leveled reader.

Read for Meaning

☐ Write about graphic sources.

School + Home **Wrap Up Your Week** Turn your paper over. Write about what you did at school. What did you read? What did you learn about people adapting?

My Work Plan

Put an ☒ next to the activities you complete.

 ## Word Wise

☐ Write sentences.
☐ List words.

 ## Let's Write!

☐ Write and illustrate a picture book.

 ## Word Work

☐ List words.
☐ Write a short story.

 ## Words to Know

☐ Define words with endings.
☐ Write sentences.

 ## Get Fluent

☐ Read a leveled reader.

 ## Read for Meaning

☐ Draw a conclusion.

Wrap Up Your Week Turn your paper over. Write about what you did at school. What did you read? What did you learn about overcoming obstacles?

My Work Plan

Put an ☒ next to the activities you complete.

 **Word Wise**

☐ Circle prefixes.
☐ Write sentences.

 **Let's Write!**

☐ Write a friendly letter.
☐ Write a response.

 **Word Work**

☐ Sort words in a chart.

 **Words to Know**

☐ Use context clues to define unfamiliar words.
☐ Write sentences.

 **Get Fluent**

☐ Read a leveled reader.

 **Read for Meaning**

☐ Make a generalization.
☐ Use supporting details.

Wrap Up Your Week Turn your paper over. Write about what you did at school. What did you read? What did you learn about animal adaptations?

My Work Plan

Put an ☒ next to the activities you complete.

 ## Word Wise

☐ List words.
☐ Write sentences.

 ## Let's Write!

☐ Write a formal letter.
☐ Include the date, greeting, and closing.

 ## Word Work

☐ Match homophone pairs.
☐ Say the words.
☐ Write sentences.

 ## Words to Know

☐ Use a thesaurus to find synonyms.
☐ Write sentences.

 ## Get Fluent

☐ Read a leveled reader.

 ## Read for Meaning

☐ Write about graphic sources.
☐ Tell information the graphic sources provide.

Wrap Up Your Week Turn your paper over. Write about what you did at school. What did you read? What did you learn about adapting to new places?

My Work Plan

Put an ☒ next to the activities you complete.

Word Wise

☐ Circle suffixes.
☐ Write sentences.
☐ List words.

Let's Write!

☐ Write a narrative poem.
☐ Capitalize the first letter of each line.

Word Work

☐ Sort words in a chart.
☐ Say the words.
☐ Write sentences.

Words to Know

☐ Use context clues to define unfamiliar words.
☐ Write sentences.

Get Fluent

☐ Read a leveled reader.

Read for Meaning

☐ Make a generalization.
☐ Use supporting details.

Wrap Up Your Week Turn your paper over. Write about what you did at school. What did you read? What did you learn about why people change themselves?

My Work Plan

Put an ☒ next to the activities you complete.

 ## Word Wise

- ☐ Circle prefixes.
- ☐ Write sentences.
- ☐ List words.

 ## Let's Write!

- ☐ Write an autobiographical sketch.

 ## Word Work

- ☐ Identify base words and prefixes.
- ☐ Write sentences.
- ☐ List words.

 ## Words to Know

- ☐ Circle suffixes.
- ☐ Define words.
- ☐ Write sentences.

 ## Get Fluent

- ☐ Read a leveled reader.

 ## Read for Meaning

- ☐ Draw a conclusion.
- ☐ Use supporting details.

School + Home **Wrap Up Your Week** Turn your paper over. Write about what you did at school. What did you read? What did you learn about how people find adventure?

My Work Plan

Put an ☒ next to the activities you complete.

Word Wise

☐ List the number of
   syllables in words.
☐ Write sentences.

Let's Write!

☐ Write a rhyming poem.

Word Work

☐ List multisyllabic words.
☐ Write sentences.

Words to Know

☐ Underline Greek or Latin
   roots.
☐ Write sentences.
☐ List words.

Get Fluent

☐ Read a leveled reader.

Read for Meaning

☐ Write about characters and
   plot.

School + Home **Wrap Up Your Week** Turn your paper over. Write about what you did at school. What did you read? What did you learn about technology and adventures?

My Work Plan

Put an ☒ next to the activities you complete.

 ## Word Wise

☐ Write sentences.
☐ List related words.

 ## Let's Write!

☐ Read a news article.
☐ Take notes.
☐ Paraphrase information.

 ## Word Work

☐ Sort related words in a chart.

 ## Words to Know

☐ Define unknown words.
☐ Write sentences.
☐ List parts of speech.

 ## Get Fluent

☐ Read a leveled reader.

 ## Read for Meaning

☐ Write about graphic sources.

Wrap Up Your Week Turn your paper over. Write about what you did at school. What did you read? What did you learn about adventures in space?

My Work Plan

Put an ☒ next to the activities you complete.

Word Wise

- ☐ Circle Greek word parts.
- ☐ Write sentences.
- ☐ List words.

Let's Write!

- ☐ Write a biographical sketch.

Word Work

- ☐ Sort words in a chart.

Words to Know

- ☐ Define multiple-meaning words.

Get Fluent

- ☐ Read a leveled reader.

Read for Meaning

- ☐ Write the author's purpose.
- ☐ Use supporting details.

School + Home **Wrap Up Your Week** Turn your paper over. Write about what you did at school. What did you read? What did you learn about exploring caves?

My Work Plan

Put an ☒ next to the activities you complete.

Word Wise

- ☐ Circle Latin roots.
- ☐ Write sentences.
- ☐ List words.

Let's Write!

- ☐ Write a letter to the editor.

Word Work

- ☐ Sort words into a chart.

Words to Know

- ☐ Use context clues to define unfamiliar words.
- ☐ Write sentences.

Get Fluent

- ☐ Read a leveled reader.

Read for Meaning

- ☐ Write causes and effects.

Wrap Up Your Week Turn your paper over. Write about what you did at school. What did you read? What did you learn about the California Gold Rush?

My Work Plan

Put an **⊠** next to the activities you complete.

 ## Word Wise

- ☐ Circle Greek word parts.
- ☐ Write sentences.
- ☐ List words.

 ## Let's Write!

- ☐ Write a summary of a book.

 ## Word Work

- ☐ Sort words into a chart.

 ## Words to Know

- ☐ Identify prefixes and base words.
- ☐ Write sentences.
- ☐ List words.

 ## Get Fluent

- ☐ Read a leveled reader.

 ## Read for Meaning

- ☐ Make a generalization.
- ☐ Use supporting details.

Wrap Up Your Week Turn your paper over. Write about what you did at school. What did you read? What did you learn about unexpected situations?

My Work Plan

Put an ☒ next to the activities you complete.

 ## Word Wise

- ☐ List words.
- ☐ Circle suffixes.
- ☐ Write sentences.

 ## Let's Write!

- ☐ Write a journal entry.

 ## Word Work

- ☐ Sort words into a chart.
- ☐ Write base words.

 ## Words to Know

- ☐ Define unknown words.
- ☐ Write sentences.

 ## Get Fluent

- ☐ Read a leveled reader.

 ## Read for Meaning

- ☐ Draw a conclusion.
- ☐ Use supporting details.

Wrap Up Your Week Turn your paper over. Write about what you did at school. What did you read? What did you learn about humans' effect on nature?

My Work Plan

Put an ☒ next to the activities you complete.

 ## Word Wise

☐ List words.
☐ Write sentences.

 ## Let's Write!

☐ Write a mystery.

 ## Word Work

☐ List words.
☐ Circle the final syllable.
☐ Write sentences.

 ## Words to Know

☐ List words.
☐ Label parts of speech.
☐ Write sentences.

 ## Get Fluent

☐ Read a leveled reader.

 ## Read for Meaning

☐ Write the main idea.
☐ Use supporting details.

School + Home **Wrap Up Your Week** Turn your paper over. Write about what you did at school. What did you read? What did you learn about things that we value?

My Work Plan

Put an ☒ next to the activities you complete.

 ## Word Wise

☐ Circle Latin roots.
☐ Write sentences.
☐ List words.

 ## Let's Write!

☐ Write a parody.

 ## Word Work

☐ Sort words into a chart.

 ## Words to Know

☐ Circle suffixes.
☐ Write sentences and base words.
☐ Write antonyms.

 ## Get Fluent

☐ Read a leveled reader.

 ## Read for Meaning

☐ Compare and contrast two stories.

Wrap Up Your Week Turn your paper over. Write about what you did at school. What did you read? What did you learn about safe travel?

My Work Plan

Put an ☒ next to the activities you complete.

 ## Word Wise

☐ List words.
☐ Write sentences.

 ## Let's Write!

☐ Write a book review.

 ## Word Work

☐ Sort words into a chart.

 ## Words to Know

☐ Use context clues to define unfamiliar words.
☐ Write sentences.

 ## Get Fluent

☐ Read a leveled reader.

 ## Read for Meaning

☐ Write statements of fact and opinion.

Wrap Up Your Week Turn your paper over. Write about what you did at school. What did you read? What did you learn about influences?

Name ___________________________________

Week of _________________________________

My Work Plan

Cross off each symbol after you complete the activity.

 **Word Wise**

 **Read for Meaning**

 **Get Fluent**

 **Word Work**

 **Let's Write!**

 **Words to Know**

Journal Writing

Cross off the day of the week after you write in your journal.

Monday   **Tuesday**   **Wednesday**   **Thursday**   **Friday**

Practice Book

Draw an X in the box when you finish your practice book page.

	Assignments	Did you finish?
Monday		
Tuesday		
Wednesday		
Thursday		
Friday		